Pocket Manual – Your quick guide to Digital Marketing

Sharing quick steps to improve your marketing efforts in the digital age
By D.P. Son
Diversity4Tech.Science

Pocket Manual – Your quick guide to Digital Marketing

Cover image: VisMe–Unsplash / Kevin Bhagat
Cover design: Diversity4Tech.Science

ISBN – 9781728929316
Imprint: Independently published

The Netherlands

About the author

D.P. Son is specialized in Digital Marketing and Event Management with working experience at international companies. Very passionate about technology and all things digital, and frequently writes articles and listicles about technology and its development.

Special dedication

To all those we always and non-stop supported and believed in me, you know who you are, especially mother, sister and late father.

Contents

Thank you acknowledgement

Acknowledgements

Thanks to everybody involved in the creation and preparation of the book. And thanks to all the readers and future readers of this book, you are the most important ones making distribution of the book possible. Your feedback, opinion and comments are welcome in order to improve next editions and to learn what topics you wish to be covered and to see us publish in.

You can send an email to info@diversity4tech.science with in the subject the title of this book and include in the email your name and email address in order to review your feedback and contact you back regarding this. Please note, your contact details will only be used for the purpose of improving the book and next editions.

Introduction

This book is a bundle of Diversity4Tech.Science blogs about Digital Marketing and modern practices. Plus, more information and data are added to provide a well-written guide that is practical and sensible for anyone interested or working in the field of Digital Marketing. All content is self-produced based on experience, knowledge, analysis of the market, and comparison of tools and practices used.

Thanks to technology, consumers became smart consumers, since everything and all kind of information can be found online, on the Internet. Consumers no longer wait for information from companies nor they need to listen what companies have to say. Nowadays, people can actively get information, reviews and recommendations about companies and their products and services, by simply using the Internet and Social Media on desktops and mobile devices.

Consumers know what they want and where they can get it best. Companies are now obliged to adjust to the needs and desires of the consumers, and not the other way around as it was before. Consumers want everything fast, easy and compact; consumers don't want to think when using online tools.

Companies need to adopt a more personal approach in their communication with consumers, and make the use of their digital tools as easy as possible for consumers. So from a marketing perspective, there is an engagement economy which entails that companies should be more engaged with consumers and their needs. For that reason, Digital Marketing is so important and plays a big role in carrying out the business activities. Via Digital Marketing you can use tools to interact with, analyze, understand, inform, and satisfy your customers better. This quick guide will help you to make a Digital Marketing strategy and plan in easy-to-follow steps, and to understand the importance of Digital Marketing in the digital age where we are currently living in.

Chapter 1 Creating a Marketing Strategy

Digital Marketing Tips and Tricks

First tip is creating a **Digital Marketing Strategy** for your business, company or project. It is very essential to know your own business, its objectives, its accomplishments, target market, target audience, potential clients and even your competitors and their Digital Marketing Strategy.

We will discuss this subject in three parts.

1.1 Creating Digital Marketing Strategy Part 1 – Analyze own business and competitors'

As mentioned above, it is necessary to do research on your own business and competitors. Once you have this information, you will have a better understanding of what drives your business, what is lacking, what can be improved, what works well with current clients, how normally clients hear about and reach you etc. This will enable you to develop a Digital Marketing Strategy.

Usage of available media
Analyze the different available media, both traditional and digital media. And conclude which means are more applicable for your business, taken into account where the most traffic of clients and new clients came from.

Once that is clear, blend the traditional media (like TV, print media, radio, newspaper, Yellow Pages, Direct Marketing) with digital media (like Display, newsletters, search engines, social media, online video, content marketing), only of course selecting the means that work best for your business and marketing goals. This blend is called Cross–Media Marketing, more on this in chapter 2 in paragraph '2.3 Introduction to Cross – Media Marketing'.

Content
After selecting the media that are best applicable, creating content is the next important factor. Make sure the content is entertaining, educational, visually intriguing, short and easy to read. Equally important is content that encourages, engages your audience / readers and connects with them by talking about their needs and not yours.

Consumer's behavior and identification
The next step will be, analyzing your current consumer's behavior when they are purchasing your services / products, and obtaining information about your business and brand. This enables you to know in which stage the consumer is.

There are different stages, these are as follows:
- Knowledge → consumer just wants to get to know the company / brand and what it offers
- Consideration → consumer is considering making a purchase
- Action → consumer is ready to make that purchase
- Usage → consumer is using/consuming the purchase made
- Experience → consumer now experiences and observes the usability of the purchase
- Opinion → consumer has a clear opinion now after the experience
- Recommendation → based on the perceived experience, the consumer will either recommend or not the purchase made

More on the different stages of consumer in paragraph '7 Consumer behavior stages online'.

1.2 Creating Digital Marketing Strategy Part 2 - Match your business goals and objectives with the marketing goals

The next step is to match your business goals and objectives with the marketing goals. After undertaking the aforementioned step in the previous paragraph, you have identified what the business goals are exactly and the means how you can reach these goals. Depending on the current business goals, you set the marketing goals.

Business goals could be:
1. Increase brand awareness.
2. Increase the number of sales (online and / or offline).
3. Increase conversion which entails that visitors of your website or in your store / office turn into buyers of your services and / or products.
4. Increase consumers' loyalty (online and / or offline).

Marketing goals could be:
1. Increase the traffic to your website or offline business.
2. Increase the quality of those visits, meaning attract potential clients that are valuable to your business (those who are likely to purchase).
3. Increase the quality of users on your Social Media, referring to users who are your target audience and feel connected with your business and its services / products.
4. Increase the engagement level on Social Media.
5. Increase the Click-Through-Rate (CTR) in Display (online ads) and e-mail offers (newsletters).
6. Improve the recognition / brand awareness of the brand or the company name.

These marketing goals should always be SMART which enable to reach the set business goals;

- Specific → be clear in which area you want improvement and what the exact goal is.
- Measurable → set a target for your goal, for example measuring if the goal is half way to be completed when the target is to e.g. increase online traffic by 20 percent in one month. Hence, the goal should be easy to measure.
- Attainable → the target should match with real results. Prior to setting the goals, there should have already been a visible and clear overview of real results and the current developments.
- Realistic → check frequently the results of what is happening in reality in order to stay realistic rather than what is ideal.
- Time-bound → set the period in which you want the goal to be reached, can be daily, weekly, bi-weekly, monthly, yearly etc.

In order to measure these goals, you can set KPIs (Key Performance Indicators) which can be for example:
- The number of unique visitors received over a set period of time (when the goal is to increase web traffic).
- The number of sign-ups received for a mailing list or to receive information (document, quote, brochure etc.) (when the goal is to increase leads and having a database of valuable customers).
- The number of contacts received via Customer Service channels (when the goal is to improve the Customer Service and sales leads).
- The number of online purchases made over a set period of time (when the goal is to increase sales).
- The number of incomplete online purchases made over a set period of time (when the goal is to increase conversion).

More on KPI in chapter 2 'Media channels and consumer analysis'.

1.3 Creating Digital Marketing Strategy Part 3 – Determine means to achieve online marketing goals

After having clear knowledge about and an overview of your company, its business goals, marketing goals, media channels, and consumer's behavior, it is possible to set the means on how to achieve the marketing goals.

Logically, the next step is to determine the means on how to achieve and to measure the online marketing goals. There are different ways to achieve these set goals. For instance, when the goal is to increase loyalty, means could be as follows:

- marketing actions on Social Media, increasing the sales number of regular customers.
- marketing via e-mail by sending out newsletters (setting up a mailing list) about latest deals and offers, only to those customers who specifically granted permission by opting in for the newsletter.

Measurement techniques

Before determining the means on how to measure these goals, you should learn about the available measurement techniques. There are two techniques, namely:

1. Qualitative; which is based on the investigator's experience of the consumer's behavior. The qualitative analytics provide you analysis of the user's behavior on your website. The methods in here are as follows:

- observation (online behavior)
- interview (for consumer's opinion)
- survey (for consumer's opinion)
- focus groups (for consumer's opinion)
- structured (for consumer's opinion)
- non-structured (for consumer's opinion)

The results are useful to optimize the navigation and improve online experience of the user (UX) on your website.

2. Quantitative; statistical tools used to predict the consumer's behavior to your website. The quantitative analytics provide you numeric analysis of the user's behavior coming to your website. This technique is used in digital marketing to get insights on how users landed on your website, via which channels (online and offline channels). These methods are as follows:

- experiments (online tracking)
- surveys (online survey how the user learn about your business)
- panel (how users learn about your business)

These above methods are conducted online with the use of suitable tools like Google Analytics, Adobe Analytics, comScore, Unbounce, Clicktale, Crazy Egg or Optimizely.

The different ways that can be determined on how to measure the online marketing goals, could be as follows by:

- Consumption; analyze the consumption of users, like purchases made, the frequency, size of purchase and type of products / services purchased (thus referring to the consumption behavior).

- Content; which keywords are used to find your website, what content is frequently read and searched for on your website etc.

- Leads; which channels generate you more leads, like providing more people that sign up for your newsletter or want to receive more information.

- Sales; analyze the volume of sales as an effect that stems out from the set marketing goals and efforts made to achieve them (the development of the number of sales online; is there an increase or decrease)

- Registration; analyze the number of registrations on your website for an online account or registering for an event / webinar etc.

Summary chapter 1 - Creating a Digital Marketing Strategy

In summary, the steps to take into account when creating a Digital Marketing Strategy are:

1. Do research on your own business and competitors (make a SWOT analysis).
2. Analyze and explore the different media options both traditional and digital, which the use of both types is called Cross-Media Marketing.
3. Create interesting, entertaining, educational and visually intriguing content that is relevant, short and easy to read. This is called Content Marketing.
4. Analyze consumer's behavior and identification, to know in which consuming stage the customer is at that particular moment and include the result in the process of setting the marketing goals.
5. Identify and understand the set business goals and the means applied to reach these goals.
6. Set the marketing goals which are SMART and include KPIs.
7. Determine the means on how to achieve the marketing goals.
8. Identify the measurement techniques.
9. Determine the means on how to measure the online marketing goals.
10. Draw up the Digital Marketing Plan and strategy.

Now you can start creating your Digital Marketing Strategy following these steps.

Chapter 2 Media channels and consumer analysis

2.1 KPI

3 steps to set KPIs:
1. analyze business goals
2. evaluate the set SMART marketing goals
3. derive KPIs from these marketing goals as a measure to achieve them

What are KPIs exactly? KPI stands for Key Performance Indicators which is a technique to measure and ensure the completion of the set marketing goals. The marketing goals support the general business goals. The first step is to analyze the business goals, as mentioned previously in the first chapter in paragraph 'Creating Digital Marketing Strategy Part 2'.

I. Analyze business goals

These goals could be:
1. Increase brand awareness.
2. Increase the number of sales (online and / or offline).
3. Increase conversion which entails that visitors of your website or in your store / office turn into buyers of your services and / or products.
4. Increase consumers' loyalty (online and / or offline).

II. Evaluate the set SMART marketing goals

The marketing goals set to increase brand awareness can be for example:
1. Increase the traffic to your website or offline business (SEO, SMO, SEM, offline branding).
2. Improve the recognition / brand awareness of the brand or the company name.

The marketing goals set to increase the number of sales can be for example:
1. Increase the Click-Through-Rate (CTR) in Display (online ads) and e-mail offers (newsletters).
2. Increase the quality of web visits, meaning attract potential clients that are valuable to your business (those who are likely to purchase).

The marketing goals set to increase conversion can be for example:
1. Increase the conversion rate by offering deals, discounts, trial, quote, or a gift which are visible during the whole website visit (surfing period).
2. Increase quality of website and / or the web shop and the user experience (UX).

The marketing goals set to increase consumers' loyalty can be for example:
1. Increase the quality of users on your Social Media, referring to users who are your target audience and feel connected with your business and its services / products.
2. Increase the engagement level on Social Media.
3. Increase customer satisfaction.

For all these marketing goals you can set KPIs to accurately measure the progress of these goals.

III. Key Performance Indicators per marketing goal

Sales, by analyzing:
- Sales per hour, daily, weekly, monthly, quarterly, annually whatever is suitable to get results of the current progress/situation;
- The average order size (average shopping bag);
- The average margin.

Traffic, by analyzing:
- Website traffic;
- The sources where traffic comes from;
- The number of unique visitors received over a set period of time;
- Amount of new visitors against regular visits;
- Total amount of pages visited per visit;
- Total time spent on the website.

Customer Service and satisfaction, by analyzing:
- Interaction level;
- Customer Service channels used to contact your business;
- Average time for solution, handling a query;
- Level of satisfaction.

E-commerce, conversion, by analyzing:
- Total amount of subscribers (e.g. number of sign-ups received for a mailing list, newsletters, deals offers, document, quote, brochure etc.);
- Level and quality of traffic;
- Social Network presence (online visibility);
- Number of incomplete online purchases made over a set period of time;
- Initiated chat / telephone sessions for instant assistance during the online purchase process.

Analytics for web traffic, by analyzing:
- Quantitative → number of users visited the website and pages;
- Qualitative → quality of those visits:
  1. Time spent on website.
  2. The (time) zone visitors are located at that particular moment.
  3. The consumption funnel, which is useful to find out for example in which phase during the buying process, visitors decide to abandon the website.

Social Network, by analyzing:
- The level of visibility;
- Level of interaction from users / visitors;
- Loyalty and engagement level:
  1. Quantity of comments and interactions.
  2. Quality of comments (positive, negative).
  3. Number of likes, mentions, shares.

All the above are also (used) interlinked when setting the KPIs for Social Network.

2.2 Online Consumer behavior stages – Discover the 7 Consumer behavior stages

There are different stages when it comes to consumer consumption. These stages are all an effect of the way consumers behave online. Due to the internet, we are currently living in a digital world, where we are experiencing a 'New Consumer' wave. This is a wave where consumers are no longer dependent only on the information provided by merchants, brands, companies etc.

The 'New Consumer' wave consists of the following two types:

1. Smart–consumer → individuals who first investigate and consult information online (desktop, laptop, mobile devices) concerning product / service, before buying.
2. Pro–consumer → consumers who pro–actively share and post information online about products / services.

These types are linked to the different consumer's behaviors that identify the stage that the consumer is in when purchasing services or goods.

Consumer's behavior and identification stages:

1. Knowledge; getting to know the company and its services / goods.
2. Consideration; considering making a purchase.
3. Action; to actually buy.
4. Usage; the moments when the purchased services / goods are being consumed.
5. Experience; how the usage is being experienced.
6. Opinion; based on the times the purchased services / goods were consumed and how the consumer experienced it.
7. Recommendation; based on the opinion, consumer can recommend or not to own network (family, friends, online reviews etc.).

For each stage, there are online marketing tools to influence the behavior.

Display, SEO and SEM can be applied to influence the following stages:
- Knowledge (except SEM)
- Consideration
- Action
- Usage

Social Media can be used for all seven stages, especially for consideration and action, 'Social Media Optimization' (SMO) is a key tool. Affiliation (via affiliate programs) is useful for knowledge and action.

These stages are influenced by the trends online which are changing rapidly thanks to technology advancement. You can leverage these trends to affect the desired customer behavior stage.

Existing trends online:
- Smartphone; can be used to further promote your services / products, where information can be sent in a direct and fast way. This includes for example a mobile-friendly website, online ads on mobile-friendly websites and search engines, a mobile app or ads on mobile apps.
- NFC; include and use technology like NFC, Near Field Communication. This enables for example payments with smartphones in shops and public transportation, and also to download coupons.
- Geolocation; can be used for restaurants, hotels, leisure, shops, offering coupons etc. especially on mobile devices (including tablets), a way to introduce consumers to your business who are close to your business' location when looking online for similar products / services.

2.3 Introduction to Cross - Media Marketing

Cross-media marketing is a blend of traditional and digital marketing media. A website is essential here and it is the main focus in marketing nowadays, which is supported by the following media:

Online media
- Social Media Marketing (SMM)
- Social Media Advertising (SMA)
- PPC →paid search marketing, part of Search Engine Marketing (SEM)
- Blog Marketing → blogging and Content Marketing
- Email Marketing →newsletters, invitations events / online deals
- Video Marketing → usage of online video platforms like YouTube, Vimeo, Instagram Video / Live, Facebook Video / Live, TEDx Talks
- Mobile Marketing → advertising via mobile apps, geolocation, mobile-friendly website and ads
- Search Engine Optimization → analyze and include trendy keywords that match your business and its products / services in your online channels to optimize your webpages and online presence
- Directory Advertising → advertising in business directories or online yellow pages for example
- Online audio → exposure for example via podcasts

Offline media
- Print Media → print like magazines or newspapers, brochures, flyers, business cards, and other marketing collateral like white papers or paper newsletters
- Press releases (can also be online)
- Trade show Marketing → fairs, events, conferences
- Radio advertising →interviews, commercials
- TV advertising → interviews on TV shows, commercials
- Products / services branding → the website address should be mentioned on each product package and service as well

All the above media channels should include the website address and an e-mail address too, to redirect consumers to your website and to easily contact you electronically.

Summary Chapter 2 - Media channels and consumer analysis

Even though, online media is important due to the digital world we are living in, offline is equally important too. When linking offline to online, you enable audience and potential users / consumers to discover your business and products / services online via your indicated website. Furthermore, when consumers hear about a certain topic via their network, TV, radio or print media (magazines, newspapers) it is likely they want to learn more about it and will look for it online. Having a website with related, relevant, and updated content is therefore very crucial. Cross-Media Marketing should be a standard element in your marketing strategy and always take into account the consumer behavior stage when performing your online marketing activities.

Chapter 3 Online Marketing channels

Social Media – 10 Best practices for Social Media usage

Here you will learn 10 best practices for Social Media usage. It is divided into 3 parts; part 1 is about the different interaction and engagement levels, part 2 is about the different social networks, part 3 is about Social Media strategy.

Social Media are online social networks like Facebook, Twitter, Pinterest, Instagram, Snapchat, YouTube, LinkedIn, and Tumblr. They are very useful tools to connect with (potential) consumers, audience and users.

Just as explained earlier in the previous chapter about consuming stage, social networks can be used for all seven consumer behavior and identification stages, namely:

1. Knowledge; getting to know the company and its services / goods.
2. Consideration; considering making a purchase.
3. Action; to actually buy.
4. Usage; the moments when the purchased services / goods are being consumed.
5. Experience; how the usage is being experienced.
6. Opinion; based on the times the purchased services / goods were consumed and how the consumer experienced it.
7. Recommendation; based on the opinion, consumer can recommend or not to own network (family, friends, online reviews etc.).

These online Social Media allow you to interact and engage with your audience in live mode. Depending on the online marketing goals set and therewith the stage you wish to influence, you adopt the proper interaction and engagement level. There are different ways to do so.

These ten best practices are as follows:

1. Manage your Social Media accurately.

2. Stay competitive.

3. Interaction with your online audience.

4. Encourage your audience to engage more on your social networks.

5. Connect with your community's / audience's lifestyle.

6. Showcase personal side of your company / brand.

7. Identify which Social Media suit what demographics and target groups.

8. Analyze and assess which social networks really work for and match your business.

9. Implement Social Media into the Digital Marketing Strategy.

10. Set KPIs for your Social Media channels.

3.1 Social Media -10 Best practices for Social Media usage part 1

In Social Media Part 1 the first seven practices will be covered.

I. Manage your Social Media accurately:

1. Engage with your audience of each social network you have an account for →
   - reply on comments on own posts published or on other posts where your company is mentioned in.
   - monitor mentions across the social network channels.
2. Expand your audience by generating leads →
   - follow influencers* of the applicable community (social network) and the posts they publish.
   - engage with influencers and followers in posts and conversations.
   - search for online conversations by keywords and hashtags.
   - increase traffic by including hashtags / tags (mentions) and geotags in your posts (e.g. in Facebook and Instagram posts).
   - discover and explore online content based on hashtags, tags and geotags.
   - engage actively with your followers on your own Social Media pages by commenting, liking and sharing.
3. Browse and check your Social Media feed frequently in order to perform all the above.

II. Stay competitive:

1. Discover insights from your competitors, other companies in the industry, individuals, suppliers or potential clients, and partners by consulting their Social Media pages and other online platforms (e.g. pro-consumers, bloggers, vloggers etc.) that include these players (competitors, partners, clients, suppliers) in their Social Media posts.
2. Discover new online trends in services / products and latest digital campaigns.
3. Communicate with customers, clients, suppliers, influencers about the launch of new products, services, events or a promotion / last-minute deal / contest etc.

III. Interaction with your online audience:

1. Investigate what your audience likes, talks about and shares online. A way to influence the interaction level and engage with the audience in a natural way.
2. Analyze your audience overall behavior and the incentives to express that behavior, habits, and opinions. This is another way to better understand your audience, in order to interact and connect with them in a natural way.
3. Convert your audience into your brand ambassadors, by:
   - rewarding them when they share your content and generate likes for your page and posts.
   - triggering them to share your content, which can be realized when your business shares entertaining, educational, lifestyle content that intrigues users. Another option is to host online contests like fan photos or videos and reward the winner.
4. Encourage employees to connect and engage with your company and its content on its Social Media pages, which will boost the interaction level of other users. Simply, because your employees have a network of their own and their network sees their online interaction in the feed, causing a domino effect.

IV. Encourage your audience to engage more on your social networks:

To have your audience watching and reading more of your content, the following could be applied:
- Encourage a specific call-to-action (a link to a promotion deals webpage, contact details to enter a contest, email etc.).
- Increase community engagement by actively engage with users.
- Acquire new subscribers for newsletters etc. with hyperlinks in the newsletter to your Social Media pages.

V. Connect with your community's / audience's lifestyle:

1. Offer visually intriguing content, layout etc. to capture attention.
2. Highlight products / services that match a certain lifestyle that the community identifies with. For example, an online subscription for wine tasting events for those who like wine and collect them.
3. Promote your company's corporate culture that portrays that particular lifestyle that matches that of your audience or those aspiring this lifestyle.
   For example, a company that has an inclusive workforce where everybody can contribute new ideas or suggestions in an open and easygoing atmosphere, can portray a lifestyle that is relaxing with multicultural diversity where everyone enjoys this and feels home. Or a company that offers sports and leisure to its employees, also in the office where there is a gym with swimming pool. This company supports sports activities and a healthy lifestyle where those pro-health users can relate to.

VI. Showcase personal side of your company / brand:

1. Provide exclusive content (photos / videos) like from behind the scenes or backstage tours, where the audience can have a peek of your office / shop or your events organized. This makes your content real, authentic and distinguishes it from the rest.
2. Provide this content in a combination of real-time and disappearing content (like Snapchat) where the published content encourages the users to want to see more which increases their engagement and devotion.

VII. Identify which Social Media suit what demographics and target groups:

There is a general understanding of which target audience and reach, each Social Medium covers.

1. Facebook → global and useful for everyone and every type of business.
2. YouTube → global, but more used by millennials and adults between 18 and 45 years old.
3. LinkedIn → targets worldwide young professionals, graduates, jobseekers, Sales Representatives, companies from every branch and partners' seekers.
4. Instagram → millennials and young adults until 35 to 40 years old, high-end influencers and celebrities worldwide.
5. Pinterest →mostly used by women, all from different backgrounds and professions ranging from professionals, bloggers, influencers, foodies etc. worldwide.
6. Twitter →global, mostly used by young professionals.
7. Snapchat → used by millennials and young adults worldwide.

3.2 Social Media -10 Best practices for Social Media usage part 2

VIII. Analyze and assess which social networks really work for and match your business:

Before selecting Social Media for your business, you should also investigate the usage of each Social Medium in your geographic area where your business is located or the local market (s) you want to reach. This will give you an insight of which social networks are actually used geographically by your target market and audience, and the way how they engaged online. Based on that identification, you can select the suitable social networks.

By analyzing and assessing each Social Medium you will learn not only the online behavior of your audience, but also the available features of each social network for more engagement and to drive more traffic.

Social Media features for engagement and more traffic:

1. Twitter:
- List → helps to keep up with users and competitors. This can be a personal / private or public list. With the first function, you can keep up with competitors' content without publicly following their profiles, or you can do research on prospective customers by gaining insights into their daily online conversations.
The public list enables you to curate accounts that might be interesting to followers such as influencers that your company is working with. A benefit of using a public list, is that users receive notifications when being added which can motivate them to check your Twitter profile.

- Likes tab →this function is visible and accessible on your profile to users, who can see what you liked. In here you can add and build a collection of media articles with positive mentions about your brand / company or products / services.

- Geotags → add location in your posts.

2. Facebook:
- Add a 'call-to-action' button to your page → like call now, send message, contact us, visit us etc.

- Add Third Parties' apps → this is good for optimizing your Facebook page. These apps could be MailChimp, Instagram, Twitter, Pinterest etc. Just choose apps that support your business objectives and marketing goals. When you send out newsletters as part of your digital marketing strategy, MailChimp in your Facebook page will allow users to opt in for the newsletter without having to leave your page.

- Add contact information and location.

- 'Like' other companies' Facebook pages that share a similar vision → a way to build community.

- Pages to watch → a feature to learn how competitors are doing it on Facebook and what you can learn from them via the likes, reach, posted comments etc. that they receive. You can check their daily or weekly or monthly audience growth, and the number of engagement and mentions they have.

- Facebook Live → you can publish live video on your page of your events, a sneak peak of your company etc. A perfect way to invite your audience to engage with the content by sharing their opinions in the comments, liking and sharing the content with their Facebook friends.

3. LinkedIn:

- Complete all information in your company profile.

- Create a company page and if necessary, display company name and description in more languages.

-Encourage employees to connect their profiles with your company page in their job description.

-Showcase pages → add this feature to the company page which enables you to market different products / services separately using target marketing, and to customize positioning and messaging. This is very useful for especially big companies.

4. Instagram:

- Add a call-to-action to your page → you can add email, call button, business address and directions.

- Use emoji's and branded hashtags → this is to emphasize and represent the aspects and characteristics of your business.

- Add website link → add the best and most appealing page of your website. This page and the whole website should be mobile optimized, in other words guaranteeing a mobile friendly usage.

- Tag others and comment on photos.

- Use statistics → a tool to measure which content resonates better with the users, based for example on the content reach, age, geographic location, time users are mostly active, gender etc.

- Instagram Live → you can publish live video on your page of your events, a sneak peak of your company etc. A perfect way to invite your audience to engage with the content by sharing their opinions in the comments, liking and sharing the content with their Instagram community.

5. YouTube:

- 'Best organized content' display → you can for example display a playlist that enables users to go from video to video.

- Channel trailer → a way to welcome new viewers and to familiarize them with your channel and company.

- Add other social networks to your channel → this will allow your viewers to engage with your company on the Social Medium of their choice.

- Optimize videos → you can do this by:
  ➢ Individual thumbnail; small images displayed on the channel page with title and description.
  ➢ Metadata, same effect as keywords.
  ➢ Clickable overlays → which are links displayed on the top of the channel page. Can maximize engagement with your viewers of your company's channel. For example, you can add annotations to drive viewers to more content on your channel.
  ➢ Add video cards → these are added at the end of your published video to lead visitors to a landing page of your website. This could be a page for more information on the topic, contact information etc.
  ➢ Branding → add this feature to your channel. It is also possible to use custom watermark with a specific call-to-action, like 'subscribe', which gives your channel a more professional look.

***Influencers:**

Individuals who are known from the public sphere, and are seen as knowledgeable about a certain topic or as an authority. They can be bloggers, vloggers, keynote speakers, authors, celebrities, politicians, etc.

3.3 Social Media -10 Best practices for Social Media usage part 3

IX. Implement Social Media into the Digital Marketing Strategy:

After selecting the Social Media channels, the next step is to set the Social Media Strategy that is in alignment with the Digital Marketing Strategy.

The Social Media Strategy can be based on:
1. Increasing customers' satisfaction.
2. Generating more sales leads.
3. Driving more website traffic.
4. Getting higher revenue.

X. Set KPIs for your Social Media channels:

Just like explained previously in chapter 2 in paragraph '2.1 KPI', it stands for Key Performance Indicators which is a technique to measure and ensure the completion of the set marketing goals. In this case, the Social Media Strategy sets forth the KPIs whereby this strategy in turn is derived from the marketing goals.

As per above goals in the Social Media Strategy, the KPIs directly associated with these can be for example:

1. Increasing customers' satisfaction → set an average time for solution and handling a query; e.g. reply back within 12 hours to 80% of the queries and 24 hours to all queries.
2. Generating more leads → increase the number of sign-ups received for newsletter via e.g. MailChimp that is integrated in Facebook; e.g. have a 10% click through of each post to generate leads by filling out the newsletter sign-up form.
3. Driving more traffic -> increase the number of visitors over a set period of time; e.g. increase followers to build a bigger community and more brand awareness by 5% per month.
4. Getting higher revenue -> increase the level of visibility and interaction from users; e.g. encourage current users to share your posts with others via incentives (voucher, gifts etc.), increasing the share level by 10%.

More KPIs for Social Media can be based on:

- Quantity of comments and interactions

- Quality of comments (positive, negative)

- Number of likes, mentions, shares -> increase engagement rate (total likes + comments + shares per post divided by followers): e.g. Facebook by 0.15 % or Instagram by 1%.

3.4 Content Marketing

The content on your website and Social Media channels should always be relevant, up-to-date, and to the point. Besides creating content for your own channels, also engage with content of others that are related to your topics. There are numerous ways on how you can be more involved and engaged with content across the internet. Here are some important examples:

- Make your content SEO-friendly so it can be easily found on the web. More on this later in the paragraph 'SEO'.

- Engage in online discussions → you can use web tools like Hootsuite, Hashtagify.me, TweetReach, and BuzzSumo to track, monitor, and analyze all engagements with your content, social media posts, hashtags, keywords, related topics and mentions throughout the internet and Social Media channels. This way you can interact and engage actively with the users on these online platforms like forums, blogs, vlogs, articles etc.

- Blogging → besides having your own blog and commenting on other blogs, you can also invite others to write a guest blogpost for you. You can also be a guest blogger for others. The point here is, the more present and active you and your business are online, the higher the chance that you are likely to be found on the web. Let's formulate it differently, if no one is talking about you and you are not writing about yourself either, how do you expect others to find you and your business online?

Blogging

Blogging should not be underestimated in your Digital Marketing efforts as it contributes to community building which enables brand awareness and growth of the engagement level. This is what you can do to increase your blog community:

1. Acknowledge and compensate → talk about other content authors/writers and recognize their work in your content.
2. Collaborate → reciprocate in likes, comments, shares and invite users as guest blogger/ writer on your page.
3. Participate → participate in the community by accepting interviews, giving ideas/tips, and be willing to be a guest blogger/writer.

Most common mistakes in blogs:
- Use of too many widgets.
- Not publishing and updating content frequently.
- Publishing too much or too little personal information.
- Creating false expectations, making promises that are not met.
- Not allowing comments.
- Use of unattractive and useless titles that do not match the content.
- Make spelling and grammar mistakes.

Some writing and content tips to make your content stand out and appealing:
1. Use narrations.
2. Write listicles. That is a contamination of the words lists and articles which refers to articles where the information is written in a list; e.g. 10 steps how to improve business. This makes the content intriguing, easy and accessible to read.
3. Give practical advice and/or tutorials.
4. Include interviews in the content.
5. Select and mention your sources used regarding a certain topic.
6. Enable reviews and ratings on your online platforms.

7. Give opinions in your content and give reviews on other platforms about a topic relevant to your content.
8. Provide space on your page for discussions.
9. Offer contests and rewards.
10. Give predictions about new emerging trends in a specific industry. This makes the content open to discussion.
11. Bring up a dilemma/problem by requesting help from users to solve a subject matter which you don't know how to solve. This will increase engagement from your readers with your content.
12. Use contact features; like contact form, call-to-action button, or even artificial intelligence like a chatbot to interact instantly with readers/users.

3.5 Video Marketing

In Digital Marketing, video is as crucial as water for human beings. Nowadays, brands cannot afford to have no video content on their pages. Why is it that important?

Videos enable your audience to learn more about your business culture, character, social voice, and your connection to the world and them. Pictures say more than words, and videos do more than that. They are part of your image building. Instead of reading about your company, users can see, hear and feel what your company is all about. People, especially millennials, want to learn about something in an easy and fast way, video makes that possible. By creating video content, you portray an image and trigger feelings that you want people to experience when hearing about your company. You want people to connect with and relate to your business and the products/services that you offer. Let's take as an example Coca Cola, when you think of Coca Cola you think of happiness and togetherness as they portray that in their advertising both print and video.

If your company is, for example, a travel agency and you want people to know that organizing trips can be done fast, easily and cheap; make that clear in your video content by including the services that make these possible. Or if your company is a foundation that helps kids in underprivileged communities to have meals at school every day, you can show in your video that you care about the wellbeing and development of your community and how positively the activities affect the children. You can do this by showing for example kids running and playing with each other with a big smile on their face which give the impression that they have energy and are happy. This is better, than to make people feel sorry as people tend to react in general better on positive feelings.

Whatever message, image or feelings you want to portray, they must have a positive effect on the audience perception about your company. Make sure, you always trigger positive emotions.

Popular video platforms to use for creating video content: YouTube, Vimeo, Facebook, Instagram, Periscope.

3.6 Mobile Marketing

All online content should be optimized, meaning that your website, blog, online ads, videos etc. should all be compatible with any device. Users no longer only use desktops to be online, on the contrary, the majority is on mobile devices like mobile phones and tablets. The more reason to make your content 'responsive design–proof'. This allows your content to be visible and available on any device and screen size, as the content will automatically adapt to the pages and apps where it is shown.

As mentioned previously in paragraph '3.4 Content Marketing', it is very important to be present and active online in order to be found on the web. By making your content mobile friendly, you contribute to that as more users are online on their mobile devices.

When it comes to online ads on search engines like Google, make sure that the campaigns are also segmented to mobile users, in order to show the ads on mobile devices too. Another important thing to keep in mind in 'Mobile Marketing', is the use of geolocation and submission of your business information to search engine business listing like Google My Business. This will help users to find your business, especially important for physical businesses like those active in tourism; hotels, restaurants, bars, shops.

In short, the three keys in Mobile Marketing:

1. Social → use content including video content where people can relate to and that can be shared easily via online channels.
2. Local → use geolocation so that people can find you as one of the nearest options where they are physically located via the used apps. You can use e.g. Google, Trustpilot, TripAdvisor, Yelp or Booking for this, where users can find your business based on where they are locally or the specific location that they are searching businesses for.
3. Mobile → the content should be optimized for all type of devices, so that it is available to users irrespective the device they are using when being online. The content for mobile devices must be short and easy to read as these have smaller screens.

3.7 SEO (Black / White Hat)

As mentioned before, make your content SEO-friendly. SEO stands for Search Engine Optimization, meaning that your content should be easy to find organically on search engines like Google or Yahoo! or Bing (main search engines) based on the used keywords by the user. Keywords are the words introduced in the search bar of the search engine by online users. If your company, for example, is delivering flowers as a service, then keywords like 'flower delivery' or 'online florist' can be used in your content in order to be found and shown in the search results.

Applying SEO in your online marketing, is the organic way to make your content findable online and provides your website a natural positioning in search engines. The other way is paid and that is done via SEM (Search Engine Marketing), more on this in the next chapter.

There are different tools available to learn more about the trendy keywords that you can use and are relevant to your content. Online tools useful to look for trendy keywords in your industry and market:

-   Webtrends.com
-   Google Trends
-   Google Search Console
-   Google Cache
-   Google Ads (formerly Google AdWords)
-   Google Suggest
-   Overture
-   Wordtracker (paid)

Also offline channels, like TV, radio, magazines and newspapers are great sources to stay up-to-date about what people are talking about currently. As people tend to search these popular topics online, when heard about them to learn more. Use these topics when relevant to your content, in order to make your content fresh, relevant and up-to-date.

SEO can be split into two components, namely:

- SEO on page → the internal factors that affect your webpages
- SEO off page → the external factors that affect your webpages

SEO on page
These are the factors that you are responsible for, and partially have a direct influence on the search results.
These are as follows:

1. Content → paramount to be original, unique, essential, good, relevant, to the point. The use of owned images, tags and metadata are equally important.

2. Structure → make the content presentable so that it is clear and easy to read (easy usability). In order to do so, you need to use and pay extra attention to the web code, domain, titles, internal links, architecture of the website (recommendable to enable navigation through the website and menu on one page, like blog style, which allows people to see all information in a flash by just scrolling, meaning less effort needed to navigate. This is also useful for the crawler robot of the search engine as it is easier to crawl your website), and a friendly URL.

3. Efficiency → showcase the content and the web pages in an efficient manner. This means you need to take into account the location and capacity of the server (choose a server nearest to your target market which influences website speed), web programming languages/sources (using Flash makes your website hard to be indexed by search engine robots), and website speed as it is recommendable to have web loading in less than 2 seconds.

4. Mobile-friendly → include responsive design and a mobile sitemap in your digital acts. In this era, more users are active on mobile devices and search often on these devices. This phenomenon can't be stressed enough.

5. Indexation → make the content easier to be indexed by the search bot by including geographic factors like location (geolocation) and different languages available. Furthermore, the programming language for the web used makes a difference in the positioning of your website in the search engine.

SEO off page
These are factors external to your own SEO efforts that influence your website positioning in search engines.
These are as follows:

1. Incoming links → redirection from an external link to your website. The links that use your URLs in their content that facilitate more traffic to your website, must be relevant, and natural. If your company sells cars, redirection from a website that focuses on beauty would make no sense. Always investigate these redirections as they influence your business' ranking.

2. Social Media → any share, comment, mention have an influence on the visibility of your company and products/services. The more people that are talking about you on Social Media, the better for your page ranking.

3. Press releases and reviews → both online and offline have influence on your ranking. When people read offline about you in press releases and reviews in newspapers for example, the odds are that they will later look for more information online to learn more. As lots of people are looking online for your business, this will increase your ranking position in the search results. The same goes for online versions of press releases

and reviews, when you are more present online, there are more sources available that refer to your business which influence your ranking positively.

4. Directories, forums, blogs → when your business is discussed by external parties in these channels, your ranking will be affected positively as more sources are mentioning your business, so that leads to an enhancement of your online visibility.

SEO objective

The general objective of SEO is to increase organic traffic to your website. This can be realized by the before mentioned SEO on page and SEO off page. The additional duties performed to do so are:

- Organic search (results from searched keywords in search engines)
- Display (banners and images)
- Direct (introducing the website link directly into the internet browser)
- Referral (engaged in affiliate marketing where affiliates can refer your business on their website)
- Email (make a mailing list where you send newsletters to users with clickable content that redirects to pages on your website)

A very important note here is, that you should always seek quality of traffic over quantity. You may have lots of traffic, but if no one is willing to spend money on your business, you should consider adjusting your Digital Marketing Strategy.

Tricks and tips for SEO management

Handling SEO is a job in its own right. Make sure that you have someone in your team that works on SEO dedicatedly. In order to manage SEO properly and with full dedication, the below activities are to be carried out. These are tips and not an exhaustive list that will grant you success automatically.

1. Build a SEO strategy, by performing:
    - initial web analysis → explore the web and online behavior of the users.
    - keywords analysis → conduct a keyword search in search engines and make a list of keywords you believe potential clients are looking for, investigate trendy keywords and use those that are applicable and relevant to your business in your content. By investigating the searched keywords you get an overview of the most used words and see the titles of the first results in the search engine which inspire you for words to use in your titles and content.
    - competitors' analysis → explore and compare the websites of the competitors, investigate their keywords, analyze their ranking and number of pages shown in search engine result pages, investigate the digital channels that they use to be active and available on, analyze their online behavior and engagement with users.
    - incoming links analysis → investigate the links where traffic to your website is coming from as this is useful to analyze your online visibility and how to leverage that. Also check from which search engine people landed on your page.
    - subscribe in search engines and directories → affects your online visibility positively (increases).
    - social network → be active on a variety of Social Media channels (only those that work for your business) as these will increase your online visibility.
    - web design and web improvement → take into account content, images, videos, web programming language, architecture, structure, mobile-friendliness, available local languages, location details, website speed, sitemap optimization etc.

- Evaluation report → evaluate all your findings and also the SEO results that all these above gave you. Based on that, you can adjust your SEO strategy accordingly to optimize your webpages.

2. **Match keywords with your content:**
   Make sure the keywords that users are looking for in the search engine match the majority of the words you use in your content and texts. Note, the average length of keywords to be used in a search is 4 words as this affects conversion rates (number of visits to your website via the results in the search engine). Less or more words can worsen the effectiveness of the search and conversion.

3. **Search for and enable online feedback:**
   Besides looking for what people are saying about you on the web, you can also allow users to leave reviews and ratings on your website, blog, Social Media pages, and review platforms like TripAdvisor or Yelp.

4. **Monitor the traffic:**
   Always analyze where the traffic to your webpages is coming from as this gives you an insight on which digital channels you could place more focus in your SEO strategy to increase your online visibility.

5. **Monitor your website ranking:**
   The website optimization efforts are to increase your ranking on the results pages, that is why it is imperative to continuously keep an eye on your ranking in order to improve your positioning.

6. **Learn ways to trick the search/crawler bot (like the Google bot):**
   Some tips to manipulate the search bots to visit your pages, are as follows →
   - repeat keywords in metatags on the page.
   - create mirror sites; thus creating similar pages (replica) of the original one in order to improve the availability and visibility of the original site.
   - search your website often to have the bot visit and index the website more often.
   - update the homepage and subpages (most important ones) frequently with new information and content (like new products, services, news etc.) taking into account the trendy keywords.
   - add sitemap and hyperlinks in your content as the bot finds more pages on your website via links on the already indexed page(s).
   - avoid the hyperlinks to open in new windows as it makes it difficult for the bot to index the page (of the hyperlink).
   - ensure enough text in your content to have the page indexed properly by the bot. And make captions for images, videos and animations in order to be indexed too. Providing video transcription is also important as it makes your online videos more searchable and accessible, boosting your video SEO.
   - use same keywords in the title of your webpage, the URL, in the heading of the content, and in the beginning of the sentence of the content/article and paragraph. Note, that excessive use of the keywords in your content will be penalized by the search engine which will disregard your page in the search results as a measure. Acceptable amount of use of the keywords is once in the title, heading and article description, and then twice in first paragraph and maybe once more in the rest of the article.
   - include texts/articles from Third Parties (with higher rankings) partially in your content and then continue with own content.
   - use affiliate marketing and sponsored content to have redirect links on pages of others that redirect to your website.
   - take into account that search engines algorithms change constantly and their policy, so consult the latter in order not to be penalized and disregarded from the search results (e.g. banned from the search engine index).

4 keys for SEO-friendly website:

1. indexable → the pages should be search engine friendly, in other words easy to be indexed by the search bot
2. usable → user friendly website, low efforts needed to navigate through your website (positive UX = user experience)
3. accessible → pages and content are accessible for bots to crawl them. The content should be available on any device (desktop, laptop, mobile, tablet), also take into account location of the user, and even availability in user's language if possible.
4. compatible → keywords match your content which is relevant, up-to-date, and appealing

1. Indexable

Your website is indexable when:
- can be found by bots of the search engines
- all the pages of your website can be searched and crawled by the search bots
- the content of each page can be read by the bot
- the search engines can distinguish the different content on your website and classify them in categories based on its relevance to the search conducted
- you employ link building and link baiting for more online present

The indexable practices can be split into two parts:

- **White Hat SEO** → the limits and rules of search engines are respected by webmasters / SEO Specialists when it comes to SEO. This means that the pages and content are kept relevant to the topic and keywords.

- **Black Hat SEO** → practices done by SEO Specialists that take advantage of the weaknesses of the search engines and misuse the relevance in the search results by tricks that manipulate the results for own benefits. One trick is for example linking keywords with your content when not even relevant to it. You might be ranked in a higher position which will drive traffic to your website, but as the content does not match and is not relevant to the search the bounce rate will be high and conversion rate low. Hence, these will be only one time visits, that do not lead to conversion as visitors did not find what they were looking for. This misleading information will harm your branding.

2. Usable

Your website is user friendly when:
- the content, structure and pages are simple, organized and easy to navigate
- keywords are implemented in the page title
- short and easy to remember domain address and URLs that are unique (not the same nor similar URLs) are used

3. Accessible

Your website is accessible when:
- tools are avoided that limit the access of bots to your pages to index them; like the use of JavaScript or Flash, and use of frames or iframes as bots cannot enter these frames to read the content
- subdomains and subdirectories are added to categorize the content on different pages on which the content is relevant to the topic
- web coding of your pages is error free (like HTML coding)
- content can be accessed from different devices which will improve its online search capability
- national domains are included like .es or .nl or .de for better positioning in local versions of search engines

4. Compatible

Your website is compatible when:
- website title and metatags are dynamic which is enabled by programming languages like PHP, Python, ASP. etc.
- clickable links are added in text/content
- sitemap is created which is the repetition of the menu main titles on each page in the below part of the page, especially on the homepage
- search bar is available on your website to conduct search within your website
- website and pages are subscribed and added to the biggest search engines, like Google My Business
- content and pages are regularly updated with new content that are up-to-date
- size of a page is lower than 100kb, important for the loading speed of the page
- metatags are used, which is a brief description of your company in which only 140 characters will appear in the search results of the search engine. This can have a major impact on the user's decision to click on your business page on the results page when comparing all pages shown on the results page. The user will obviously click on the ones that look more appealing.

Chapter 4 Online advertising

SEM

In the previous chapter, it is explained what SEO is and its importance to make your business as visible as possible on the web. SEO is the organic way to be findable in search engines and SEM is a monetized method to make your business findable.

SEM stands for Search Engine Marketing and is paid advertising in search engines pages. This can be sponsored links in search engines like Google which are shown on top and/or below of the search results as 'Adv.' or shown in Google Shopping.

When implementing SEM, you create advertising campaigns for your business to promote for different reasons. You can use it for brand awareness or to increase sales etc. When advertising on Google, you can use Google Ads, formerly Google AdWords, to make your advertising campaigns.

4.1 How does it work?

You determine your budget per day/month and to which demographics and in which locations you want your ads to be shown. The total costs that you pay per click (PPC), depends on the bid you placed on keywords in the Google Ad Auction. Ad Rank is your ad's position in search results in comparison to competitors using similar keywords. Well, this does not mean that, the higher you bid, the higher your ranking in Ad Rank to have Google showing your ads more frequently and in higher position than competitors'. This is merely one of the factors, that affect your ranking. Other factors are relevancy of your content to the searched keywords, use of ad extensions like sitelink or callout, and the quality of your landing page. The best matching ads appear alongside the search results.

The landing page, which is the page where your ad is redirecting to, is very important as it affects your Ad Rank, cost per click (CPC), and position in the ad auction. Poor quality and user experience of your landing page result in showing your ad less, and thereby lowering your ad's position or not even showing your ad at all.

Tips for high quality content and landing page:
- Content should be unique, original and useful.
- Landing page must be relevant to the ad text and keywords.
- Transparency about your business, openly share information.
- Easy-to-find contact information.
- Have products and services description available.
- Make landing page easy to navigate on PC and mobile devices.
- Make loading time of landing page fast (2 seconds preferably).
- Keep improving mobile-friendliness and speed.

Google Ads channels for online visibility

When using Google Ads, the system allows your ads to be shown in the following channels:

- Google search results → thus visibility on the results pages, showing your ad with text and clickable link.
- Partner websites via Google AdSense → visibility through affiliates/publishers of the Google AdSense program like blogs, content websites where your image or text ad can be shown based on the relevancy of the content.
- Google Sites → YouTube, Blogger, Gmail showing your image ads.

4.2 Benefits SEM / Google Ads

1. Management of your own campaigns → connecting with target audience where, when and how long you want. As it is segmented advertisement, you decide the geographic areas you want your ads to be shown. You can also easily modify your ads to suit your strategy anytime.
2. Control of your costs → decide your budget and you can stop the campaign anytime you want. Hence, you decide when and how much to invest in campaigns.
3. Evaluation performance of Google Ads to improve your SEM performance → keep track of the total impressions (people who saw the ad), total clicks on your ad (Click-Through-Rate; CTR) to visit the website, total clicks on the call-to-action button in the ad (call or email), and the influence of the ad on your online sales as a direct result.

4.3 SEM Management Tools

There are tools available to manage campaigns, like DoubleClick Search / Search Ads 360, the so-called search campaign management tools. They are useful to manage large search campaigns for different brands / companies. Some features available with these tools:

- Management of search campaigns with high average spending per month (in thousands)
- Management of campaigns on multiple search engines like Google, Yahoo!, and Bing
- Management of large number of keywords
- Frequent bid changes available
- Carrying out promotions frequently
- Tracking conversions across multiple channels

Tips optimizing SEM campaigns

Optimizing or improving your ad campaign is just like improving your content and landing page quality. Below more concrete tips on how to optimize the SEM campaigns exactly:

1. Segmentation → when goals and objectives are determined you can start segmenting your market, which is through the next points below.
2. Geographic area → determine the target areas for your ad campaign, so the ads can be shown in these areas.
3. Time slots → analyze which time and days of the week your ads get more conversion, in order to know when the ad campaign should be shown with more intensity.
4. Devices → analyze which devices (PC, mobiles) are used more often to search certain keywords/topics and when exactly. This way you can focus on which devices the ad campaign should be shown more often during specific periods/time.
5. Improvement tools → analyze and follow-up on the implemented tools to improve performance. For Google the tool is 'Google Ads' with its available features to create ad campaigns and to optimize these.
6. Message usage → the ad should transmit your message clearly, attract users' attention, and also make sure that you launch the proper message in the ad.

7. User suitability → Always offer campaigns that are suitable to users, keeping in mind mobile users too. To offer your users the best experience, you should think like a user on how the experience should be like (e.g. access a relevant and useful page that loads fast).
8. Stand out visually → make the ad noticeable and attractive for users, e.g. using bigger space on the screen.
9. Advertisement extensions → add value to the ad by using extensions. These enable you to add more information to your ad like a sitelink, and your ad has more visibility as it is larger and takes more space on the screen to advertise.

Types of advertisement extensions

You can add different kinds of extensions to your ads, depending on the suitability to your business and the action required from users when seeing your ad. Examples of these extensions are as follows:

- Website links extensions / sitelink → to add more links to your ads (specific pages on your site: like store hours or products page), which are visible on the bottom of the ad, thus as the last line.
- Callout extensions → to add additional text with more detailed information about the business, products / services to make it more noticeable. This can also be used to promote offers and deals.
- Geographic location extension → add an address and / or map.
- Call extension → add a call extension to have users call you directly from their mobile devices.
- Application extension → add an extension for mobile devices when you want users to download your app.

4.4 Why SEM campaigns

As a conclusion SEM can be performed, as long as the ad campaign is profitable for your business. Profitability can be measured as follows:

- Getting qualitative traffic to the landing page to reach the set goals/objectives; like increased conversion and sales rates.
- Increased brand awareness; the branding and image of the brand is enhanced.
- Increased ranking in search engines.
- Strong coordinated actions with SEO efforts; where the campaign aids the improvement of your position in the search results.

Chapter 5 Web analytics and digital marketing tools

5.1 Web analytics

The goal of performing web analytics, is to optimize the usage of the company's website. Web analytics give you lots of information about your online performances, enabling you to improve these performances and optimize your website.

Purpose and usefulness web analytics:

1. Allows seeing the number of page views and unique visitors →useful for calculation of conversion rate and lead generation. These can be the total number of purchases made or newsletter sign-ups.

2. Analysis of demographic factors, like location of users → useful to better understand your clients, the markets and which are more important for your business and to put more focus on. In other words, to identify and better target your audience.

3. Analysis of users' behavior → you can analyze how users behave on your website, like pages visited and time spent on it. This is useful to understand the effectiveness of your website and its content on reaching the marketing goals, e.g. increase sales, leads or increase the spending of customers etc. The measurement of effectiveness stems out from your set KPIs, which allows you to analyze the level and progress made from the implemented tools and see how you are actually performing to reach the goals.

4. Overview of the online sources from where users landed on your webpage → useful to know and understand which sources and platforms are mostly responsible for generating more traffic to your website which you can use in your strategy and also as potential channels to actively engage with the users. These sources can be search engines, blogs, websites, forums, e-magazines, Social Media, apps.

5. Analysis of the effectiveness of tools used to generate more traffic and/or sales →this allows you to see the results of your efforts done to reach the marketing goals. These tools can be SEO, SEM, Social Media Marketing (your channels), Blog Marketing (your blogs) etc. Now you can decide which tools are more effective in reaching the set goals and where improvement is needed. This also allows you to stay up-to-date about the latest trends concerning online world and technology to understand the shift in users' behavior of using available online tools and channels (before Facebook or Skype as very trendy, now more Instagram or WhatsApp).

Types of web analytics

There are two types of web analytics where a distinction can be made, namely:
- Quantitative
- Qualitative

Quantitative analytics:
This is the numeric analysis of users' behavior coming to your website.

Qualitative analytics:
This is the analysis of users' behavior on your website. The information acquired, is useful to optimize the navigation and experience of the users on your website.

Web analytics steps

When doing the analysis, there are a few focus points that help you on how to do the process. These are as follows:

1. Plan → clarify what you want to measure.
2. Implement → determine the tools necessary to measure the above.
3. Measure → use the tools to measure the numeric findings and results in order to have an overview.
4. Analyze and observe → use the tools to make observations, segment and understand the web developments and online users' behavior.
5. Interpret and report → document and verbalize the analysis in order to make decisions and strategies. Translate the observations in clear, sensible, useful and relevant words to base conclusions on.
6. Optimize → use the decisions and strategies made to make improvements, and optimize your online present and effectiveness on reaching the business goals.

Web analytics challenges

Web analytics comes with some challenges too. Though, it is paramount for your business to perform analytics, but it is not as easy as it sounds. The big challenge that you face, is the data management. Obtaining the data is not the difficult part, but interpreting these data adequately and making the right decisions from these to optimize your channels, are challenging.

Some tips on how to handle data:
- Process all the information separately from each other.
- Put related data together to make decisions.
- Take the time to make proper decisions and keep in mind that results take time too.

Web analytics tools

There are tools available to obtain online information, measure and process the information. The tool that makes it possible for your online channels, like website and Social Media pages, to obtain information concerning users' online behavior, is cookies. Cookies enable you to get this information needed to be analyzed in order to optimize your online channels. Note, that users should be warned that you use cookies on your website which they can accept or deny. And your use of the cookies should be in accordance with the General Data Protection Regulation (**GDPR**), in force since 25 May 2018 by the European Union to guarantee data protection and privacy for all individuals within the European Union and the European Economic Area, and safeguarding the personal data for export outside of these areas.

As addressed earlier, depending on what you wish to measure, you can determine the tools. Therefore, you should always keep in mind before selecting the proper tools, your business objectives, business budget, and the measurement focus. The latter refers to quantitative and qualitative analytics, where each of these have their own available tools.

Quantitative tools

The tools available are as follows:
- Google Analytics
- Adobe Analytics
- comScore
- Quartcast
- Webtrekk
- Webtrends
- Clicky
- Woopra
- Coremetrics
- Matomo (formerly Piwik)
- Audiense (for Twitter)
- LikeAlyzer (for Facebook)

Qualitative tools

The tools available are as follows:
- Unbounce
- Clicktale
- Crazy Egg
- Optimizely
- Visual Website Optimizer (alias VWO)

5.2 Online Reputation Management (ORM)

Another important information to know, that is useful for your Digital Marketing Strategy and tools management, is your online reputation. Not only brand awareness is important in order to have people visiting your website, driving more traffic to it, but online reputation is equally important as it influences the willingness of users to use or continue using your products or services. Therefore, your company should focus on Online Reputation Management too.

ORM implementation

ORM should be handled with care, especially in an online crisis. Your company is always responsible and accountable for any communication between your company and users. For this reason, it is imperative to show users that you are actually listening to what they have to say to you, you are correcting your errors, and are learning from negative feedback / criticism in order to improve your communications and reputation. Steps for ORM implementation:

1. Determine the possible damage.
2. Understand and show understanding to affected clients.
3. Respond properly and respectfully to the online attack.
4. Protect your company's brand and image; offering some sort of compensation to affected clients when feasible.
5. Be always transparent.

ORM channels

ORM can be measured amongst others by consulting the following channels:
- Forums
- Blogs

- Social Media
- Online news platforms
- Reviews and ratings (own website and external websites)
- Websites in your niche community (websites that operate in the same niche, being part of the niche community of active users)

ORM tools

It is not easy to find all the above channels to learn what people have to say about your company and your Customer Service, good or bad, and to track these feedback and mentions. Luckily, there are digital marketing tools available to enable you to track any mentions, opinions, reviews, shares etc. Some available tools to monitor the web for content:

- Google Alerts
- Hootsuite
- Mention
- Alerti
- Hashtagify.me
- TweetReach
- BuzzSumo

Channels for loyalty creation

Besides managing your reputation via interactions, you can also create and enhance customers' loyalty. Channels enabling you to do so, are as follows:

- Email marketing
- Social Media
- Newsletter (to update subscribers about new developments, promotions, products etc.)
- Remarketing (remind visitors to visit your website or download your app via display ads)
- Mobile Marketing (geolocation, ads in search engines, ads on mobile-friendly websites and apps)
- Exclusivity via granting access to clients only, like special events or gift for loyal customers etc. as VIP
- App (encourage users to download your app for more information and special deals etc.)

5.3 Digital Marketing tools

Depending on each digital task performed there are tools available, like those for web analytics, content monitoring, SEO, SEM, affiliate marketing, Social Media management, and also customer relationship management (CRM). CRM lets you manage your company's interaction with current and potential clients, through interactions via online contact form, email, chat, Social Media, surveys etc. This is to help you gather data and make analysis about clients' relations and history with your company to improve business relationships with them.

The tools available for the first four digital tasks, are already pointed out in previous chapters. Here are some recommendable available tools for affiliate marketing, Social Media management and CRM:

Affiliate marketing programs (managing your online ads and appearances on publishers' channels or monetizing your website with ads from advertisers)

- Rakuten LinkShare
- CJ Affiliate
- ShareASale

- Amazon Associates
- ClickBank

Social Media management (managing your Social Media accounts from one platform)

- Hootsuite (free basic version)
- Buffer (free basic version)
- Crowdfire (free)
- Sprout Social
- eClincher
- Agorapulse
- SocialPilot (useful for teams and agencies)
- Sendible (built specifically for agencies managing Social Media accounts of several clients)

Customer relationship management

- HubSpot (free basic version)
- Salesforce

Now you are all set and ready to create your Digital Marketing Plan with suitable strategy. And it is okay to make mistakes as this is the only way to learn what works for your business to reach the goals. Good luck and enjoy!

– End –